Finding Czarinaty

The Journey To Peace Through Cancer And Chaos

CZARINA LYNELL

Finding Czarinaty

Published by iCHAMPION Publishing

P.O. Box 2352 Frisco, TX 75034

Content edit by Charmaine Patterson and iCHAMPION Publishing

Library of Congress Cataloging-in-Publication

Data Publisher and Printing by iCHAMPION Publishing

Cover design by iCHAMPION Publishing Design Team

Finding Czarinaty, The Journey To Peace
Through Cancer

And Chaos

ISBN: 9 78-1-7349212-0-5

Autobiography

Christians- Religious Life, Self-Help Printed in the United States of America

Finding Czarinaty, The Journey To Peace
Through Cancer and Chaos

Czarina Lynell

This book is a memoir. It reflects the author's present recollections of experiences over time.

Locales, physical properties, occupations, and places of residence may have been changed, some events have been compressed, and some dialogue has been created.

Names of individuals have also been changed as well as identifying characteristics and details to protect their privacy and identity.

He said to her, "Dear woman, you are made well because you believed. Go in peace. You will not suffer anymore."

Mark 5:34 (ERV)

Dedication

This book is dedicated to:

My Husband, John A. Matthews, II

My Children, Justin Matthews,

Jaecin Matthews, and Javen Matthews

My Sister, Catina Laverne Smith;

AND

My Nieces, Canisha LaChelle Smith,

Aijah D'nae Smith, Triniti Gibson

I have written this book in Memory of:

My Mother, Cora Lynn Smith

My Mother-in-Love, Vera Lee Matthews

AND

My Aunt, Alice Schnell Smith

Acknowledgments

Thank You God for your vision, your strength and your healing power to be able to write my story and share it with the world. I would like to thank my family and my friends for their love and support throughout this journey. I would like to thank Stanley McAllister for being a messenger for God and communicating His prophetic word.

I want to thank my Sponsorship Angels:

Mr. & Mrs. Michael Bussey, Rev. & Mrs. Frederick Taylor, Mr. & Mrs. Gregory Cole, Mr. Donnie Walker, Mr. & Mrs. La Zette Smith, Mr. & Mrs. La Zette (D.J.) Smith, Mr. & Mrs. Alvin

Matthews, Mr. & Mrs. Drewkai Butler, Ms. Linda Walker, Ms. Amanda Walker

I want to thank my Sponsorship Heroes:

Shamilah Ivory, Cathleen Abriam, Brandee

Davis, Tanisha Griffin, Jackie Pugh, Misondri

Smartt, Tahar Vinson, Brittany Bray, Kristen

Channel, Ladybug Media Management, Shanta

Tyiska, Sharene Acosta, Antionette Green, Mr. & Mrs. George Sapp, Janai Hoston, Loran B Anderson, Jennifer Johnson

Organizations and Individuals who pushed me through to the finish line:

iChampion Publishing, HerGrind HisGlory, AJ Joiner, Sharai Robbin and The Literary BAE Academy

I want to especially thank those who were a huge support, during my treatment journey:

Cortez R. Smith, Sr., John A. Matthews, Sr., Catina Smith, Cortez R. Smith, Jr. (Dana Clarin), Canisha Smith & Family, Aijah Smith & Family, Triniti Gibson, Sahnjae Oliver, Jahari Oliver, Gwendolyn Walker & Family, Carl Walker & Family, Benicia Harris, Roberta (Momma Berta) Thomas & Family, Mr. Darrell Matthews & Family, Mr. Marlo & Mrs. Dawn Smith & Family,

Mr. Flemmie & Mrs. Dana Rolling, III & Family, Mr. & Mrs. Cory Walker & Family, Ramone Burrell & Family, Ida Johnson, Charmaine Patterson, Missionary Temple C.M.E. Church Family, Pastor Sheryl Brady, Bishop Joby Brady and the entire Potter's House of North Dallas Family, Dr. Phillip A. Kovoor and Texas Oncology Staff (Plano, TX), Dr. Meghan Hansen, and Dr. Joshua Lemmon.

Last but certainly not least, I want to thank the ones who have endured it all and have been with me every step of the way throughout this journey - my husband and my children, Justin, Jaecin, and Javen. Thank you for loving me through the tough times and really living out our vows – for better or for worse. You never left my side and for that I am grateful. Thank you for being my friend and my protector.

I love you!

CONTENTS

Preface

"Don't be afraid of not being perfect, it might be what makes you amazing."

— Jolene Stockman

The world is hurting. We are a hurting generation, suffering inner turmoil that has caused many of us to suffer health issues physically, mentally, and emotionally. Many of us think we *have to be strong*. We saw our mothers and our grandmothers – Madea and Nana, exude their seemingly supernatural strength daily, and we now hold ourselves to the same standard. We put so much pressure on ourselves to be Claire Huxtable, Harriet Winslow, and Vivian Banks. We aspire to be the high producing, money-making, food preparing picture of the modern-day virtuous woman. For most women, this perfect persona is unrealistic and hard to maintain.

This memoir was written for those women - the many women, like me, who have spent a lifetime painting a picture of perfection while silently suffering. We are needlessly suffering because:

1. We refuse to admit we have a problem - we feel shame, guilt, or embarrassment.
2. We refuse to talk about it - worried about what others will think or say.
3. We refuse to get help – too busy telling ourselves that we *don't* have a problem.
4. Some of us are too prideful.
5. Some of us believe mental health issues don't exist at all.

This will continue to mentally hurt us, especially – as black women. After we push ourselves to the limits of being everything to everyone: a wife, mother, sister, daughter, auntie, grandmother, mentor, employee, and friend; we will eventually become overwhelmed with those responsibilities. Before long, we find ourselves suffering from the *S.A.A.D. Woman Syndrome*, (becoming a Stressed, Anxious, Angry, and Depressed Woman). We try to carry out the legacy of strong women in our families, not realizing they may have been suffering too – they just never talked about it.

It's time to talk about it. It's time to take a deeper look into the woman in the mirror - not the woman we show everyone else, but the woman behind the mask. What is revealed when we take the mask off might be scary and maybe even traumatic. However, true healing begins when we find the courage to face our fears, learn from our experiences, and embrace our imperfections. Rather than trying to conceal our flaws, we must love ourselves enough to uncover and accept them for a better future. And yes, wanting better for ourselves will require change. However, instead of focusing on the pain of change and fearing the process, we should concentrate on the benefit of the end result.

It's time that we stop kidding ourselves and help ourselves. We can only heal what we choose to reveal. After years of suffering silently, I finally had to face the woman in my mirror - the woman behind my mask. My self-reflection revealed layers of unresolved Stress, Anxiety, Anger, and Depression. It wasn't an easy task, but a necessary one.

My hope is that by revealing my journey to find PEACE through Cancer and Chaos, you will find the courage to begin your own.

CHAPTER 1

Identity

"Knowing yourself is the beginning of all wisdom."

- Aristotle

While dealing with breast cancer, I was forced to come to the realization that I was an angry woman, and for good reason - or at least I thought. Nobody listened. Nobody cared as much as I did. Not only was I an angry woman, but I was someone who was very stressed and anxious. I even had a period in my life where I was depressed. I was the typical S.A.A.D Woman (Stressed, Anxious, Angry, and Depressed).

After coming to the realization that I was easily frustrated, stressed, and constantly worried about things that were beyond my control, I discerned it was time to make some changes. I knew that in order to survive, I needed to get control of my thoughts and emotions. I realized that how I think ultimately affects how I feel. Lord knows I've had a hard time controlling my thoughts and emotions over the last few years. Nine times out of ten, my thoughts led my emotions down a road I never intended to travel.

This enlightenment, during my cancer treatment, prompted me to do some self-reflecting. Particularly, I reflected on who I was, where I'd been, who I had become, and where I was going. Daily, I asked myself, *who am I?* Turns out, the answer was in the name that was given to me before I ever existed.

Who am I?

My name is Czarina, the same name as the

Russian Queen of the Czar – peaceful, calm, and serene. If ever asked what my name means that would be my reply. Internally, I believe I am a queen, but the way I've treated myself over the years, you couldn't tell. Throughout my life, I have made many decisions based solely on the needs and expectations of other people, completely disregarding my own desires, passions, and happiness. Because I have a serving heart and want everyone in the room to feel happy, I tend to make decisions that are beneficial for others. However, in the long run, it is detrimental to me.

The addiction of pleasing others and being concerned about how people will react or what they will think of me has been damaging for my own mental, physical, and emotional health. My natural inclination is to coach and support others, but I have always struggled to motivate myself. There are a lot of dichotomies ingrained in my identity. For example, I am super sweet but easily frustrated. I can be a romanticist, yet a realist. I am strong, yet very sensitive. Somedays

I feel like I have it all together, but other days I'm a complete mess! It's funny how my name implies peace and serenity, but part of my life has been nothing but chaos.

The Matriarch Effect

Like many of us women, my first role model and example of a woman was my mother. She was strong and fierce. My mom was the one who would say through clenched teeth and tight jaws, "If you don't get yo behind off of my couch"! Then turn around and feed us some of the best fried chicken, cornbread dressing, greens, and mac n' cheese you ever tasted, for dinner. She would pop my brother in the head with pots and pans or whatever she could get her hands on at the moment of feeling disrespected. My mother had zero tolerance for negative attitudes and behavior. There was no smacking of the lips, rolling of the eyes, or talking back in my house growing up. And anyone who stayed the night went to church with us on Sunday morning, whether you were a member of another church or not. Momma Cora made sure everyone went to church. She was not only my mother. She was my counselor, my loudest cheerleader, and long before she gained her heavenly wings and entered the pearly gates, I viewed her as my friend.

Before starting a family of my own, I used to think my mom was angry because she would yell *all of the time.* As a young child and even a teenager, I remember thinking, *'Why is she so angry'*? I didn't want to grow up imitating some of the characteristics and behaviors she displayed. Don't get me wrong, my mom was sweet as pie, but she was also easily frustrated. Maybe it was fear – fear of us getting in trouble outside of the home and her not being able to help us. Maybe it was the worry of us growing up without respect for ourselves or our elders. Maybe it was the thought that if we were not listening to her, we would not know how to listen and follow the law as we grew older. She wanted order, and she in fact, held our family together. However, on the inside, she was slowly falling apart.

Whatever the circumstance or root of her anger and disappointment, she could not contain it or control it. The unmanaged stress and anger festered into a myriad of physical health challenges. However, I believe my mother suffered from worry and stress even more than her actual ailments. The amount of stress that consumed her was far beyond what she could control, yet she never sought out help and help never found her.

My Aunt Alice endured a similar plight, but her disease was breast cancer. Watching the struggle of these strong women in my life, and how stress compounded their illness, I tried to live my life differently.

Once I learned their diseases could be genetic, I constantly had the thought in the back of my mind – *one day that could be me.* I saw firsthand the effects stress could have on one's health, contributing to congestive heart failure, heart attacks, renal failure, and cancer. All I could think was how stress plagued the women in my family and how it correlated to devastating illnesses and diseases. I thought about how they lived their lives and how they interacted with others. I wondered, I feared, I dreaded it happening to me. Sure enough, just a few years later, it did.

CHAPTER 2

The Diagnosis

"The thing I feared has come upon me; what I dreaded has happened to me."

Job 3:25 (NIV)

A Birthday Gift Like No Other

On February 26, 2018 - my 38th birthday - I received the news that I have the Big 'C' - Breast Cancer to be exact.

It was the moment I had been dreading all weekend during my trip to Austin with my husband and best friend. I remember the conversation like it was yesterday.

OBGYN: 'The biopsy of the lesion located under your left armpit came back positive for breast cancer.' ME: 'Ok. What are the next steps?'

OBGYN: 'Ok?' (Surprised at my response) ME: 'Yes, what do we need to do next?'

OBGYN: 'Well, I have already referred you to a breast specialist and her office will be calling you to set up an appointment. We are going to do whatever she recommends.

I didn't want to break down. My mind told me to be strong and get information about next steps. I'm convinced it was designed by God that I would receive that phone call with my husband and best friend by my side.

I immediately thought about all of the "What ifs". *What if I don't see my children graduate from high school and college, or see them get married? What if I'm not around to provide support to my children and help with my grandchildren? What if I get so sick from the chemotherapy treatment that my husband has to take care of the children and handle all of the daily activities by himself? What if I stayed in California and didn't move to Texas - would I have been diagnosed with breast cancer?* Those thoughts alone made tears roll down my face. As I stared out of the passenger-side window, my husband grabbed my left hand, and we rode up the highway in silence.

I reflected on all the stress, anxiety, and depression I have endured over my lifetime, and even more so in recent years. I couldn't help but wonder if neglecting my stress contributed to my breast cancer diagnosis. I thought about my mom who had her own issues with stress and my aunt who was also diagnosed with breast cancer. I thought about all of the times

I imagined being in this very situation – receiving a diagnosis of some illness or disease due to stress.

When we reached our rest point, we pulled over at Buc-ee's gas station to use the restroom and grab some snacks. We all got out of the car moving as if we had just been hit by a truckload of bricks. Our faces were long and showed obvious despair. As we walked towards the entrance, my BFF stopped and turned towards me. She reached out and gave me one of the most heartfelt hugs – squeezing as tight as we could in that embrace. As she pulled away, she looked me in my eyes and said, "We're going to get through this."

It was a long, quiet ride back to Dallas from Austin. By the time I made it home, I had put on my big girl panties, wiped the tears from my tired puffy eyes and put a smile on my face, for the kids - after all, it was Mommy's birthday.

To Work or Not To Work? That is the Question

I started to wrap up the day and lay my exhausted, overwhelmed body down for the night. Thoughts of my job crept into my mind. I wanted to contact my employer, but irrational thoughts filled my head.

Should I attend the 2-day seminar for work tomorrow, or should I stay home and deal with the news I had just received? Will they think less of me for calling in, after taking days off to celebrate my birthday? If I need to take time off to focus on my treatment, would they hold my position? Of course not. In that moment, I could feel the butterflies in my stomach, the uneasiness of my breathing, and the thumping of my heartbeat. As my anxiety expounded from the mere thought of becoming unemployed, I decided not to call my employer. Oh no! I didn't want them to think less of me for calling into work. I attended the two-day seminar; despite the emotional turmoil I was trying to control. For the next two days, I got up and put on my happy go-lucky mask - smiling but avoiding all eye contact for fear the slightest interaction might cause me to break down into tears.

When I made it back to the office on Thursday, I knew it would be just for a few moments – long enough to drop the bomb on my colleagues that I had been diagnosed with breast cancer. As we stood in the stillness of the small huddle room, the tears flowed, and they said how sorry they were to hear the news. I took a deep breath and told them I was leaving for the day. The comforting hugs and words of encouragement gave me the strength I needed to walk out of our building and down to my car, without bursting into tears. If I ever questioned how they felt about me, it was confirmed at that moment - they truly cared.

After my short visit to the office, I returned home and worked for the rest of the day – sending emails, conducting investigative interviews for employee relations issues, and facilitating conference calls with managers I supported across the organization. It's a shame I still felt obligated to prioritize my job above my health. Once again, I thought of others, before thinking of myself, despite the severity of my diagnosis.

To Walk by Faith or Walk in Fear

The next day, my husband and I were scheduled to meet with a breast specialist. I had been in constant prayer while preparing for my first appointment. I was extremely scared and didn't know what to expect. Although I was scared to death, my prayer was that God would go before me, set an atmosphere of healing, and bless the doctor with wisdom. I was insistent on having a double mastectomy, before even meeting with the doctor and without knowing all of the details. I planned to take an aggressive approach in my battle against cancer. I figured for me to have a fighting chance of survival, it meant removing both breasts to get rid of cancer and avoid recurrence.

As my husband and I got out of the car and walked toward the entrance of the medical building, I felt a sense of strength. We entered the cool, brightly lit doctor's office just a few minutes prior to my scheduled appointment. There was an older couple seated in the waiting area and I wondered if the woman was a cancer patient. I walked past the couple to check in at the registration desk. I could feel them staring at me as I took my seat. When I sat down, I felt out of place because I would generally relate cancer with older people. Yet there I was, at the age of 38, waiting to have my first consultation for breast cancer.

When my name was called, my husband and I quickly popped up from our seats and headed towards the Physician Assistant, who walked us back to the medical exam room. As we waited for the doctor to enter the room, my anxiety started to work its way through my body, causing the feeling of nervousness to infiltrate my chest and my stomach. After a few short minutes (that felt like forever), the doctor entered the room. I remember thinking, "*Oh my goodness, she is really young; I really hope she knows what she's doing.*"

After the formal introductions, we jumped right into the reason I was sitting in her office on that day. I told her that it was just a few months earlier that I first discovered a hard, cord-like vein protruding from my left breast. It was one of the worst days I had in a long time. Here's the story:

I had a really long day at work. I stayed late to complete a few projects. By the time I made it home, it was pretty late in the evening. My husband was out of town for work, so our children were left in the care of family members. As I walked through the door, I could sense something was not right. The house was quiet, and the kids were sitting down instead of running around as usual. I went to put my work bag and purse down in my bedroom. I checked in with the kids before they went to bed for the night and learned some very disturbing news – my then four and five-year-old partnered up and attempted to carve a pumpkin. I couldn't believe what I was hearing. From the looks of the pumpkin, there was a lot of carving that took place.

When I checked with the adults in the house, nobody could tell me exactly what happened. Then I was told I needed to find childcare for my children. I was enraged! There were six people in the house and nobody could tell me how my children managed to get a knife, climb up on the tall chairs surrounding the island in the kitchen, and begin cutting in the pumpkin. My blood pressure skyrocketed as anger and anxiety set in. All I could think about was what if one of my children cut themselves or stabbed the other.

The vision of my children covered in blood made my head hurt and my heart ache. I felt as if I couldn't leave my children in the care of family members. I was so livid, my breathing became labored and I couldn't get rid of the banging, treacherous headache. I had reached my limit of chaos in my home. At that moment, I hated my living arrangement. I was so overwhelmed with anger and anxiety, I remember thinking, *what if I broke some glass and slit my wrist?*

I knew at that moment I needed to calm down. So, I went to take a shower. As I started to undress, I noticed pain in my left breast. As I removed my bra, I felt a painful tinge as the watermelons hung low. When I looked down, I could see what appeared to be a vein about 3inches long sticking up under my skin. When I touched the area, it was hard and painful. That was the night I knew it was breast cancer.

I had done some research on the hard cord-like vein, and when it didn't go away after a few days, my husband encouraged me to make an appointment with my OBGYN. During the appointment with my OBGYN, I explained what I experienced the night of the pumpkin carving and pointed out the area. The doctor conducted a breast exam and discovered a lump under my left armpit. At the end of the appointment, she told me she'd like me to have a mammogram. The mammogram led to a biopsy of the lesion under my armpit, which confirmed invasive ductal carcinoma, most commonly known as breast cancer.

After listening to my story, the breast specialist explained how breast cancer originates in the breast and that we needed to find the 'primary spot'. This would give her a better idea of the stage of cancer and how to move forward with a treatment plan. She conducted a thorough breast exam to find any questionable areas. As she suspected, there was a lump in my left breast that I hadn't discovered. She asked me to feel the spot and asked if it felt weird to me. I said, 'yes'. She immediately made the decision to do an ultrasound of the spot right there in the exam room. The spot showed up as a cluster, but it didn't stand out as the shape she was used to seeing. She knew it was worth getting a second opinion and decided to contact the radiologist right away and asked him to review the results of the ultrasound. She sent him a picture of the image via text message for an immediate response.

The radiologist then called her to discuss his findings. In his eyes, the cluster was not one that resembled breast cancer. However, my doctor was not satisfied. Her initial thought was to schedule me for an MRI to get a better look at the lump, but there was something that wasn't sitting right in her spirit. As she was exiting the exam room, she turned around and said "I think I want to do a biopsy." As scared and nervous as I was - the spirit nudged me and said, "Tell her to do it."

And without pause, I said confidently, "Yes, let's do it."

The doctor returned to the room with all of the necessary tools needed to conduct a biopsy on my left breast. She stuck me with a long needle that contained numbing medication. As I sat up, slightly leaning back, she made an incision about an inch in length. I couldn't feel pain from the cut she made, but I could see the blood gushing out. She inserted a tool and turned it on. It began to make a weird grinding sound as it went in a circular motion, cutting out a piece of my breast tissue. As she extracted the part of my breast in question, she placed it on the testing dish and prepared it for the lab to test. She advised she would contact me with the results and if it was what she suspected, she would like me to start chemotherapy within the next two weeks.

The doctor took her time explaining everything and listened very intently to my story about how I discovered issues with my breast. She was super sweet and sensitive to my needs and feelings. She made me feel so comfortable. I walked away feeling confident in her level of expertise and ability to care for me. I thank God I didn't have to go through the trouble of finding another breast specialist and surgeon.

I had planned to return to work the following week. However, by the end of the appointment, there were so many decisions to be made and so much information to review. For a moment, I felt crushed. It was as if someone slammed a mirror against the concrete ground and it shattered into a thousand pieces. I felt overwhelmed, so I began to pray. That prayer gave me the strength I needed to face the next steps. I was determined to prioritize myself and not return to work until we knew for sure what the treatment plan involved.

By the time I returned home from the appointment, God assured me that I would have everything I needed to fight the battle ahead. I envisioned myself HEALED in the Name of Jesus! Undeniably, this fight would require another level of faith. My journey to total and complete healing was going to be the fight of my life.

CHAPTER 3

The Treatment

"Sometimes, when I say "I am ok", I want someone to hold me tight, look me in the eyes, and say "No, I know you are not."

Paulo Coelho

The Traumatic Side-Effect

When I first started my cancer treatment, I continued to do life as "normal." It didn't take long for my new normal to become my reality. I experienced pain, grief, loss, and neglect. Some days were more painful than others. Some nights were restless. A few people showed up to support my family and I, while others I expected to show up, didn't show up at all.

Within the first month of chemo treatments, I put a lot of energy into convincing myself and everyone else that I was fine. I planned and coordinated a wedding, attended a bridal shower, hosted a birthday party, helped my husband launch his catering business and continued my day-to-day tasks. Oh, and I lost my hair!

The day I lost my hair was one of the most traumatic memories of my journey. I purposely made plans to have my haircut by the boys' barber sooner rather than later. However, my husband was not in agreement with my decision to chop my hair off so soon. He didn't understand I was trying to do damage control and avoid an emotional breakdown. My intentions were good. I wanted to avoid the shock of actually seeing my hair fall out. At the time, I never thought that he may not be ready to see his wife without hair.

I followed through with my plan to have the barber come to our house to cut my hair. As I prepared for the big reveal of my new look, I thought, *I need to wash my hair.* My hair had been covered up by a wig, so I wanted to take off the wig and wash my hair, before my scheduled appointment with the barber.

I took the wig off and began to unbraid my hair. And the very thing I was trying to avoid was happening right before my eyes. As I sat on the bench at the foot of our bed, I lowered my arm to take a break from unbraiding my first braid. I looked down at what appeared to be a big, round, black cotton ball. My heart dropped. I jumped up and ran into the bathroom and stood in front of the mirror. As I continued to take my braids out, chunks of my hair were entangled between my fingers and with each stroke, patches of hair effortlessly left the scalp on my head and fell into the bathroom sink. By the time I finished taking down my braids, all was not lost. I had enough hair on my head to get a really nice low cut. So, I proceeded to wash my hair. I should have left it alone. My hair continued to slide right off of my head. I was devastated. I had plans to make sure I didn't experience this moment, but God had other plans. I had no other choice but to cut off my hair completely.

My appointment with the barber was scheduled for the very next evening. Prior to this day, I tried to prepare my oldest son as best as I could for what was about to happen. I was really nervous about how he would feel and how he would react. So, I did the one thing I thought would help make the transition of my new hair-do (or no hair-do) easy for everyone, including myself. I took a trip to the makeup store to get my face beautified, before the big chop. I figured if I had on makeup and a nice pair of earrings, my new bald look wouldn't look as bad. I remember thinking, *I can't believe I am going to be bald.* Yet, I was determined to embrace my new look, boldly. I also remember thinking, *I wish I had someone in my circle of family and friends who was bold enough and willing to cut their hair in support of my fight against this horrible disease.* For a split second, I became very nervous, but when the barber arrived, I brushed it off and pulled myself together.

Bold, Bald, & Brave

The inaugural haircut happened in the bathroom. Only the barber, my husband, and I witnessed the initial cut. Guess what? I loved it! I kept looking in the mirror, checking my angles. I couldn't believe the image staring back at me had absolutely no hair, but I wasn't the only one with a new bald look. My husband cut off all of his hair too! My mouth dropped wide open – totally taking me by surprise. I was beyond grateful for him making the sacrifice and taking a stand to support me. Before walking out of the bathroom to reveal our new look to our family, I hugged my husband and held on to him tightly. I literally felt the weight and pressure disappear.

Everyone seemed to accept the new look, with the exception of my children, as expected. My two youngest sons busted out laughing when they saw mommy's bald head for the first time. They thought it was the funniest thing. After an hour or so, my youngest son said, "Ok, you can put your hair back on". He had no idea mommy would be without her hair for a very long time. My oldest son was completely stunned when he saw my new bald look. He literally had no words. After a few minutes, he said, "You look pretty".

My hair is not the only thing I lost during treatment – I lost a very dear aunt, and a month later, I lost a very dear uncle. I lost my energy. I lost my appetite. I lost feeling in my fingers and my toes. I lost more than half of my breasts. But I never lost my faith.

Although my son said I looked pretty with a half-smile on his face, I knew my son was not ok. One month later, the school nurse called and said Justin wasn't feeling well. He had chills, but no fever, and he didn't eat lunch. So, we picked him up from school. The minute he walked in the house, he fell asleep – crashed right on the famous bench at the foot of our bed. Later that evening, Justin slowly entered our bedroom, dragging a blanket behind him. He climbed onto the bed, laid his head on my leg, and covered his face with the blanket. Before I could ask what was wrong, he asked me, "Why do you have to have cancer?"

I immediately sat up in the bed. I couldn't even begin to imagine the courage it took for him to *ask* the question. I had no idea what he was thinking or feeling, but I knew I had to give him my full attention and allow him an opportunity to speak openly and freely. My son felt something was not right and he thought enough to come to me directly and talk about it. My heart ached for my nine-year-old son who was trying to process my diagnosis and the effects of my treatment. I told him to climb up in my arms and I held him.

I said, "I am strong and I am going to fight with everything in me to beat this." He said, "Mom, I'm scared." I held him tighter and told him "It's ok to cry." In the midst of the body pain and the heartache I was feeling, I reaffirmed God was going to heal me. I tried my best to reassure him there's no need to worry so I said, "I got this!" I told him to repeat after me and together we said, "We got this!"

My husband did not agree with me confirming my cancer diagnosis with Justin. However, Justin had been thinking about it so much, he told his teacher. I know this because there was a note on Justin's behavior calendar for the day that read, "I am praying for you." I refuse to allow my child to suffer in silence. I know all too well how it feels to suffer alone. I'd rather have the conversation to give Justin an opportunity to speak freely and share whatever was on his mind. My son was hurting and worried, which was enough for me to want to push through the battle even more.

I Have Cancer – Does Anyone Care?

I was used to pushing through. I had always pushed through and supported others. Yet in this moment, I needed someone to be strong for me. I needed a safe place to just let go. I needed more love, more attention, more affection, more hugs, and more kisses. In the first half of my treatment, there were days I would wash, dry, fold, and put clothes away. I would climb the stairs to clean the boys' room and make their beds. There were many days I stood in pain to cook my own breakfast, lunch, and dinner.

Some days it was a struggle to simply take a shower and put on my clothes.

I recall one day I was so drained and fatigued from the chemotherapy, I literally laid on the bathroom floor, after taking a shower. It took me almost an hour to get my body clothed and my face painted with makeup. This was almost a daily task, getting up and dressed, to avoid *looking* sick to my children when they arrived home from school. Of course, there were days I wanted to lay in bed and do absolutely nothing.

Yet, my concern for the emotional well-being of my children wouldn't allow me that luxury.

Yes, I walked around appearing to be strong for the sake of my children, but it gave everyone else in my household the wrong impression. Even on the days I would clearly say *I don't feel well* or *I'm having a hard day* – nothing changed. Nobody stepped up. So of course, I continued to push through as if I was not a cancer patient going through chemotherapy. I felt like things were going to fall apart if I did nothing. So, being sick was not an option for me.

There were nights I couldn't sleep because my mind was racing or I was drenched in sweat. Other nights I was upset about the lack of attention I was receiving. I had been begging for attention for quite some time. I *needed* attention. One night, I asked my husband to hold me, but after an hour, he ended up falling asleep. I was so hurt. I felt worse when family came to town to help out and check on us. I think my husband was so relieved, he literally checked out. Instead of allowing the family to take care of the children and give us a break, my husband ran to the store with them, cooked with them, and hung out for half of the night with them. The following night, I was so upset because he had been gone all day. Yes, even as an adult, I will admit that I may have been a little jealous that others had my husband's attention. But don't I have the right to want his attention?

My emotions got the best of me, and I became angry because I felt neglected. I didn't want to see, touch, or hear my husband. So, I grabbed a blanket and a pillow, and I slept on the floor inside of our walk-in closet. I don't know how many women battling breast cancer would choose to sleep on the floor inside of a closet. Some may say I had an adult temper tantrum, but the closet was my safe place.

When I was diagnosed with breast cancer, my husband never really slowed down to process it all. He continued doing life as he knew it – getting the kids up and ready for school, went to work, picked the kids up after school, cooked dinner, and took Justin to football practice as Dad and assistant coach. He would then turn around and volunteer all day at church. Some days I felt it was a struggle for him to hold me, look me in my eyes, and say "I love you". I was hoping that one day he would say, "My wife is battling breast cancer. Let me focus on giving her the love and attention she needs."

All I needed was for my husband to hold me, hug me, kiss me, love me, and even talk to me. But he wouldn't. He actually never said a word about how my diagnosis was affecting him. Like many men, my husband didn't always communicate how he felt. So, I can only imagine that he felt overwhelmed with his many responsibilities. He may have felt added pressure to ensure our family remained secure. He may have feared losing his job. He may have feared losing me to breast cancer. All of this coupled with having to care for a loved-one battling cancer, while carrying the weight of an eight-person household, had to be too much for one person to handle. Yet, he managed his responsibilities the best way he knew how. Real men will ALWAYS step up to the plate to ensure their families are taken care of. Yes, sometimes this means other priorities, obligations, and even relationships may suffer, but only for a short while. So, I told myself, *I am the one who was diagnosed – not my husband, not my children, not my family, not my friends. God chose me for the journey. He chose me to be a walking testimony for His glory.*

A Shift

In the summer of 2018, I underwent a successful breast surgery, as no indication of cancer was found in my body post operation. Two days after surgery, my husband and I along with our boys, drove down to Louisiana to attend my uncle's funeral. I was afraid to travel the short distance so soon, but I didn't want to miss the homegoing celebration. So, there I was, in Louisiana with bandages across my chest.

One night, I stayed in the hotel room by myself, while my husband and the boys went to grab dinner. Shortly after they left, I began to feel nauseated and started to get a banging headache. I felt light-headed. I was so scared. I remember getting up and pacing the hotel room floor, praying. I asked God to heal my body and remove any doubts and thoughts of defeat. By the time my husband and the boys returned to the hotel, my headache was gone and I felt a lot better. Thank You Lord - I was able to get a little rest that night. The next day, we wrapped up our weekend trip and returned to Texas.

After our short trip to Louisiana, my husband packed up all of our belongings by himself, and we moved out of my father's home – the home we helped build. The home my father said had been purchased for me and my family. The home where we selected the floor plan, the cabinets, the tile, the granite, and the flooring for every room in the entire house. Yes, we left it all behind, but it was necessary.

Allow me to share a little back story. Between 2015 and 2018, my family and I lived with my father, my sister, and my niece. There was a total of eight of us in the home - three different households living under one roof. Each household lived by a different set of rules and expectations. This drove my husband crazy and I don't blame him. However, I became stressed and overwhelmed, because I was in the middle of it all - my husband on one side and my family on the other.

Even after having many discussions and conversations with my family members, nothing changed. As a result, tensions began to rise within the home and my husband's frustrations grew. As he became more frustrated, I became more stressed. So, when I was diagnosed with breast cancer, I had a conversation with my father and my sister. I simply told them, "I love you, but I don't love living with you."

Eventually, the time had come for us to have our own space. It was imperative to change our environment for the sake of my health and our sanity. A few family members tried to talk me out of it. Some even called me crazy. However, if they only knew the amount of stress and chaos we endured over the last few years, maybe they would understand. Even if they didn't understand, I knew what *I* needed to heal.

When we moved into our 4-bedroom, 4-bathroom, second-floor apartment, I truly believe that is when things began to turn in my life. Shortly after we settled into our apartment, the third and final phase of my treatment process began. My husband and I traveled to the doctor's office together, every weekday. We would wake up, feed the kids breakfast, get them dressed, make their lunches, take them to school, and head to the doctor's office.

After a few weeks, a shift began to take place. When I tell you my husband showed up – he showed up and showed out in more ways than I could have ever asked. He started working from home and became my personal driver, my personal chef, my personal everything. He never missed an appointment (for chemo or radiation). I felt like it was against the world. We spent so much time together. We talked more and laughed more. It was as if God designed the move to the apartment while having radiation treatments, so we could focus on each other. We grew closer than we had been in years. My husband played such a vital role in the final phase of my treatment journey, as he made sure I had everything I needed.

I knew my husband loved me and has always loved me. However, I had to remind myself of this one thing: just because I want him to be more affectionate does not mean he loves me any less. Yes, I wanted more, and I will not apologize for wanting to *feel* loved. However, I will apologize for how I have reacted in the past in response to feeling lonely and neglected.

I spent a lot of time focused on everything I felt was not going according to *my* plan, rather than concentrating on all of the things that were great and moving according to God's plan. I was so focused on the negative, that I became negative. As a result, the negativity infiltrated throughout my family and into my household. Eventually, I felt like my life – my family, my children, and my marriage - was spiraling out of control. I knew it could not stay that way. I could no longer function in chaos. I loved myself too much to allow that to continue.

Somewhere between the start and the end of radiation, I had a mental shift. I began to focus on healing and filtered out all negativity – negative thoughts, negative feelings, and negative reactions. I focused on the positives and channeled the peace God had given me. It was time to take accountability for my part in every aspect of my life, and vow to become a better me – a better wife, a better mother, a better daughter, a better sister, a better aunt, and a better friend. The peace that engulfed me during my cancer treatment journey is a feeling I loved and wanted to hold on to forever. In order to do that, I had to revisit childhood experiences that may have negatively impacted my life for many years.

After the radiation treatments, it was time for true healing to begin. Knowing stress would hinder the healing process, I was determined to release the chains of the SAAD Woman Syndrome that had been holding me hostage for the last few years. I didn't want to only heal from breast cancer. I wanted to heal in all areas of my life, which meant taking a deeper look into my past to help me understand my stress, my anxiety, my anger, and my depression.

CHAPTER 4

Seeds Of Anxiety

"Our anxiety doesn't come from thinking about the future, but from wanting to control it."

-Emily Francos

As I was going through my treatment journey for breast cancer and preparing for the start of my healing process, I spent many days watching the news – specifically the coverage surrounding the Me Too Movement. The news coverage sparked the courage within me to finally come to terms and deal with traumatic experiences from my past – starting back when I was a child.

My mind traveled back in time to my elementary school years - a time when I became an aunt at the age of five-years-old and was no longer "the baby" of the family. My thoughts raced back in time when I made up a story about being kidnapped because I felt neglected and needed attention, yet I was too young to articulate how I was feeling.

I thought back to the time I wanted to be friends with the popular fly kids, also known as the cool kids. Typically, they were also the kids who liked to push the envelope and challenge authority - you know, the kids who like to test your patience - the rebellious ones. They were willing to do anything to get attention, and they didn't mind getting in trouble for it. And I was willing to do anything just to be considered a friend. I was gullible, naïve, and had low self-esteem, so it didn't take much to influence or persuade me. I was an easy target to be picked on, bullied, and talked about by family members and friends.

Loss of Innocence

I was five years old when a close friend of the family used my weakness, innocence, and ignorance to their advantage. This was an older, male family friend. For the purpose of this story, let's call him Bob. Bob made me feel like we were friends. He talked with me. He played with me. He made me feel so comfortable around him that I trusted him. We shared secrets - deep, dark secrets. After all, he was like family. My family trusted him so much they often left us alone together. I now realize, having so much alone time with Bob, who I believed was my only friend at the time, was not a good idea.

Out of all the times we were left alone, I can clearly remember one instance when he manipulated me into using my mouth to satisfy his loins. I remember the musty smell. I remember the hair in my face. I remember him telling me to "lick it like a popsicle".

There were many encounters where he asked me to satisfy his little sex-crazed fantasies. Other times, he placed my hand in his pants and told me to "rub it". He used to tell me to keep "what we did" a secret. I did just that because he was my friend. I felt Bob loved me. He cared for me and played with me. I also kept our encounters a secret because I didn't want to get in trouble. Even at the age of five, I knew what we were doing was wrong because we could only commit the acts when no one was around. But Bob was not the only person to manipulate my innocence growing up. I was also violated by a few older, female family friends – in my parents' car, at church, and at home. They would use my little fingers to travel to places they never should've been. But even as a child, I cared what others thought and how they felt about me. I was a people pleaser. I just wanted people to like me and show me some attention. I had no idea I was being molested.

It wasn't until after my breast cancer diagnosis and the widespread coverage of the momentous Me Too Movement, that I finally took the time to deal with the traumatic experiences of my childhood. Over the years, I blocked out those memories. I somehow managed to get through life as if I never experienced the molestation. However, I was ready to accept it, heal from it, and move on. Emotionally and mentally, it was a rough process. At that time, all I could think about was the many times my body was used for someone else's gratification and how I never should've allowed such acts to occur. I felt like a dirty, torn rag that had been stomped on and dragged through the filthy, trodden streets of life.

Overwhelming Anxiety

Over the years, I developed severe anxiety. Some days I would get the nervous uneasy feeling in the pit of my stomach just from the thought of making a phone call, sending a text message, or even sending an email. Other days, I'd be so anxious I couldn't sit still. I have experienced the feeling of anxiety so much, I have been unable to complete a simple task because I spent too much time thinking about doing it perfectly – not wanting to make a mistake. I spent too much time overthinking and worrying, rather than actually completing the task at hand.

After my third pregnancy, I started to worry about everything. This is when my anxiety began to spiral out of control. I worried about the stability of my family, the stability of my job, my children's future, and most of all, I worried about getting breast cancer, because my aunt had it.

My anxiety grew as I feared for the safety of my children. I feared that one day my children - my young African American Kings - would fall into the hands of an unjust system. I have worried myself sick trying to raise my children in such a way that they would not fall victim to the systemic racism running rampant in our country today. I feared that my children would be looked down upon by their teachers and miss out on opportunities only afforded to their Caucasian peers. I feared they would not be able to survive independently, if they didn't excel academically at school. As a result, I began to parent based on my fears.

The Anxiety of The Past

I’ve discovered my parenting skills are a mixture of my parents’ teachings and my experiences. When watching my children play, I tend to overreact when they are playing with each other. I can’t stand the sight of them rolling around on the ground. I become very apprehensive – fearing the worst and I end up yelling from a place of rage, telling them to stop. It's all because I’m afraid of them violating each other’s personal space. Part of me knows they are just trying to play. They’re not even thinking about what I have conjured up in my mind. Yet, I worry about inappropriate touching, because it's what I experienced as a child. I wouldn't want my children to endure that same trauma. I make it a point to talk to my kids about respecting people and their space and keeping their hands to themselves. I also make sure I am very clear when I say nobody should ever touch their private areas and they should never touch anyone else's.

My childhood experiences held me hostage and planted roots of extreme anxiety and fear. Today, I am intentional about extracting those negative roots and creating healthy communication with my children about their friends and experiences. My husband and I are careful who we allow our children to spend time with. God made parents, guardians, teachers, and caregivers to watch over and protect children who are unable to protect themselves. As parents, we must talk to our children and let them know our job is to protect them from all harm, including people who may seek to violate them.

We must remember that our children are just children. They are growing and still trying to figure out this thing called life. They don't have all of the answers and they are depending on us, their parents, to guide them, believe in them, push them towards their purpose, and most of all forgive them. Oh my goodness – I have just received a revelation and have been set free even in writing this. Thank You God for your promises and your assurance. Just as our Father in Heaven forgives us of our sins and looks beyond our faults to see our needs, we should do the same for our children. We have to remember to be gentle and have compassion when speaking to our children and disciplining them. We have to remember to extend grace just as God extends grace to us each and every day.

CHAPTER 5

Stress - The Silent Killer

"My belief is that cancer comes from inside you and so much of it has to do with the environment of your body. It's the stress that will turn that gene on or not."

-Melissa Etheridge

We've heard it before – stress has the ability to take over our lives and quite frankly, end it. The hormones that are released throughout the body when we are feeling stressed can contribute to health problems such as heart disease, diabetes, high blood pressure, ulcers, and other severe health problems. Stress hormones can also have psychological effects, causing mental illnesses such as anxiety and depression. Therefore, we cannot afford to ignore the signs of stress, especially when the stress level is far beyond our control.

Stress – A Familiar Companion

For most of my life, I have been a stress-filled person. I know I may not have always appeared that way on the outside, but I have always had an internal struggle with stress. I'm not referring to acute stress – the short-lived, temporary kind of stress. I am referring to the type of stress that has a much longer lasting effect.

As I look back over the years and I analyze the most stressful moments in my life, I realize the cause of stress was attributed to family or finances. I have stressed over my parents' marriage, my relationships with my siblings, my children's behavior and development, my marriage, and my household family dynamics. The burden of stress has been a familiar companion.

There have been times that I felt as if stress had me by the throat, continuously dumping my head underwater and holding it there. The weight of the pressure was so heavy, dark, and grim – I couldn't see my way out. I didn't want to talk about it because I didn't trust anyone enough to understand. Perhaps, I was too afraid of being viewed as weird, crazy, or sensitive. Sometimes the burden of being stressed seemed easier to bear than the courage it would take to actually confront the stressors. Instead, I would become silent, distant, and guarded – a very ineffective way to manage stress.

The Stress of a Teenager

I can recall a time growing up when I was stressed about my family. I was hurt, embarrassed, and ashamed over the breakup of my parents' marriage. I was hurt because I could see the shame and humiliation my mom felt. I, too, felt shame because we had just become another statistic. My mom had become a single mother and I became a child growing up without her dad.

The atmosphere at home was so strained and so full of tension that I never wanted to be there. Music was my escape. I was a member of our high school choir, which gave me time away from home and an opportunity to do what I loved - sing, dance, and perform. However, when I was home, I would lock myself in my room with the radio blasting to escape my reality. I would switch between 106.1 KMEL or 102.9 KBLX. If Aaliyah, Brandy, Monica, Mary J. Blige, Zhane, Brownstone, Lauryn Hill, Jodeci, or Boyz II Men was playing, you could hear me singing along trying to match my voice with theirs – drowning my sorrows and covering up the pain. Other times it would be Janet Jackson, SWV, Xscape, Kelly Price, Mariah Carey, Shai, Shanice, Case, Carl Thomas, or Baby Face helping me to forget about my troubles at home as their songs inspired thoughts of hope and love. Even after witnessing the separation of my parents, I was still a hopeless romantic.

Exploited and Violated

As a teenager, I was so infatuated with the idea of love and romance. There was one young boy I was really crazy about. I wanted him to love me, and I wanted his attention. In exchange, I gave him my body. I was so nervous and intimidated. I really didn't want to go through with it, but I did. He had me sniffing so far up his nuts that I allowed him to exploit my ignorance and expose my body in the backseat of a car, while his best friend was driving. He had his finger in my pants and I felt so violated. But I ignored it because I wanted him to know how much I *loved* him. Mr. Master Manipulator manipulated me into not telling a soul about our sexual encounters. Turns out, he was telling everyone. There I was, a young teenage girl, looking for love in all of the wrong places.

During this time, I felt particularly disconnected from my family, which made it much easier for him to take advantage of me. There was something missing at home – a void. So, I tried to fill that void by putting my attention into people who were not worth my time. I just wanted to be loved. So, I compromised my Christianity to create my own sense of security. It left me feeling so guilty, ashamed, and unworthy.

Stressed & Unmotivated

As a young teenage girl witnessing the heartbreak of her mother, I still felt the pressure to remain the caring and reserved daughter, the diligent honor roll student, and the cool friend. Yet, after my father left, I was unable to focus on the one real job I had - school. I was so stressed, I didn't want to eat most days. I became anorexic. Eventually, the stress I endured manifested itself into a health issue for me. One day, I was in so much pain. I remember telling my mom, "It feels like someone punched or kicked me in my stomach." This was the only way I could describe the horrible, aching feeling. I could feel the pain throbbing right below my sternum and at the very top of my abdomen.

The pain continued for at least an hour. So, we headed to the emergency room at Kaiser Hospital on Geary St. I can remember that day in the hospital so vividly. Blood was drawn and an X-ray had been taken. We had been there for a while and after a lot of tears and testing, the doctor told my mom that I had a small case of ulcers. I had no idea what that meant. I just remember the doctor advising me to stay away from soda (especially brown sodas), hot sauce, and medicines like Aspirin. At the age of 15, stress had already manifested into ulcers - something I would have to deal with for the rest of my life.

Stress also caused me to be discouraged and uninspired in school. The stress due to my dysfunctional family dynamics became so overwhelming, I almost didn't graduate high school. Although I was literally failing every class, with the exception of Choir and P.E., I was determined to graduate. I owed it to myself and my family to finish strong. I knew I had to change my environment, if I wanted to successfully finish high school.

My teenage mind made a decision to move out of my parents' home. I came up with a plan to go live with my Godparents for a while. I made a conscious choice to remove myself from an environment that had been pulling, tugging, and eating away at my self-esteem, my joy, my peace, and my happiness. I was unsure of how my mother would respond. I knew she was dealing with the separation from my dad, and I wanted to help her - I just didn't know how. I felt so helpless. I didn't want my mom to feel like a failure. The decision to move away from home and leave my mom was one of the toughest decisions I've ever had to make, but it was the best decision. If it had not been for my Godparents allowing me to come live with them, I don't think I would've graduated.

Stress Over Finances

As an adult, married and degreed, I didn't think finances would be a real issue. Yet, for years, even with two incomes, my husband and I struggled. There have been times we would forego the items we desired to ensure our children had what they needed. We would sacrifice haircuts, manicures, pedicures, and massages. A few times, we sacrificed purchasing necessities to make sure our children had a roof over their heads and food to eat. Our finances wouldn't even allow us to take family trips, vacations, or even family photos. The thought of not being able to cover my medical bills for my breast cancer treatments was enough to keep me up at night.

There were many times when my lack of financial resources made me feel like less of a woman.

Why? Because there are certain things most women need to just help us feel good. We like to get our hair and nails done, our eyebrows arched, and our eyelashes done to make us feel special. The absence of these things seems to cause a negative cyclical effect. If we fail to take care of those basic needs, we often feel inadequate or like we are not presenting our best self. If I don't feel good about myself, I tend to lose confidence. I may even have low self-esteem, which then affects how I live my life, the choices I make, and how I react in certain situations. It's a vicious cycle.

Growing up, I never imagined myself in a situation where I had no money in savings and not enough money in my bank account to go on a date with my husband. I never thought I'd be confined to my house because I didn't have enough money to buy gas to take a ride down the highway or treat my family to a nice dinner. For years, it had been a real struggle not to be able to really enjoy life due to the restrictions of our finances. I imagined my husband and I would be hosting dinner parties, owning our own business, and traveling the world. Instead, my family has endured more financial stress than success.

I've always said I didn't want to live a life full of stress and worry, like my mother, but there seemed to be no escape. Feeling stressed, anxious, angry, and depressed were emotions I just couldn't seem to control. I had a real wakeup call the night of the pumpkin carving - that night I nearly broke some glass and slit my wrist. I realized my stress was out of control due to frustrations and failed expectations.

CHAPTER 6

Frustrations & Failed Expectations

"Expectation is the mother of all frustration. "

Antonio Banderas

The Pressure of Keeping Up

We can plan out our lives for the next 10-20 years based on what we believe and what we want for ourselves, but there is no way to avoid 'life' from happening. We can try to control our own destiny, but the reality is, only God really knows our true purpose and has the power to control our future. Oftentimes, the dreams, visions, and aspirations we have for ourselves are derived from what we learn from societal norms.

I have depended on society far more than necessary. I know I'm not the only one who has ever had an unhealthy dependence on society. Some of us depend on society to tell us what success is and what it looks like. We depend on society to tell us what a loving marriage is supposed to be. We even depend on society to tell us whether or not certain behaviors are acceptable.

Depending on what we focus our attention on, the information can possibly invade our mind and spirit and even shape what we believe. We then put pressure on ourselves to try and meet the standards of society rather than striving to meet our own. As a result, we begin to worry and stress about our future, our marriage, our children, our jobs, and our health. None of us ever actually strives to be a failure, right? None of us want to be labeled as such, either. Let's be honest – we depend on society to paint us a picture and then we desire what we see. However, the more we desire what we see, the more we find ourselves adding undue stress and pressure to live up to society's standards. This is where I believe anxiety sets in. We start to think about our current situation and compare it to the future we want, which feels so out of reach.

What happens when we try to be successful the way society says we should be - but we fail?

The pressure of demonstrating success throughout our life can become all-consuming. The idea of being successful, by society's standards, sets us up to have unrealistic expectations. These expectations & frustrations manifest in our lives, emotionally, mentally, and physically. Emotional stress can cause us to be distant, uninterested, and mute. Mental stress can cause us to think less of ourselves and have negative thoughts about life. Unmanaged frustrations & expectations can also lead us to emotional breakdowns and depression. In order to overcome the frustrations & expectations of this world, we must live by our own set of standards.

Could it be that my stress was spiraling out of control because I was overwhelmed and too concerned about how my life didn't appear to have the *look* of success?

Many of us women will go to the extreme to protect our identity, our reputations, our character, and even our family. Some of us have added responsibilities in an attempt to meet the expectations of others and refuse to ask for help because of pride. We will take on any and every challenge, obstacle, or issue just to prove we can manage it all. As women, we often suppress and carry the weight of our problems without resolve, while being a wife, a mother, daughter, sister, friend, and counselor to others. Many times we find ourselves doing this to prove our strength to those who only value their own personal agendas, rather than being truly concerned about our emotional, mental, and physical well-being. We carry the weight of everyone else's problems that we don't believe our problems are equally as important.

Many of us go our entire lives believing being strong means suppressing our pain, heartache, and grief. Some of us think strength means to support our husband's dreams and forget about our own. Others believe being strong means managing the household while holding down a job, nurturing and raising children, and serving as the family counselor and advisor. The reality is, we are often so busy operating in our many roles, that we ignore our needs. When we suppress our needs, we compromise our happiness and frustration develops. As for me, frustrations and failed expectations turned into depression.

CHAPTER 7

Deep Dark Depression

"Depression is, in part, grief for your own life not turning out how it should; grief for your own needs not being met. "

Johann Hari

After years and years of stressing about things that were out of my control, I became depressed. I would describe depression as the feeling of melancholy and gloom that lasts too long. We all get sad at times, but when the feeling of sadness and dreadfulness lingers for months, depression then becomes a sickness that needs to be treated. Many of us are walking around depressed, but we can't even recognize our own depression because we have operated in this state for so long.

Silence Isn't Always Golden

I often refer to my depression as a really dark moment in my life. I remember noticing the difference in the way that I felt about myself, my marriage, my children, and my life as a whole. For years, I lived in a constant state of unhappiness. It was hard for me to smile or laugh about simple, funny things. I was always upset, over analyzing, and judging every situation and everybody. I felt alone and lonely even when others were around. I was easily annoyed and became frustrated the minute my expectations were not met. I didn't even want to go to church- one of the few places that I really enjoyed. Depression had really set in.

Some mornings, while riding to work with my husband, I would stare out the passenger side window in complete silence. All the while I was thinking, "If he loves me, he will at least say something... Shouldn't he know how I'm feeling? Can't he tell that something is wrong?" After all, he wouldn't be okay with us not speaking at all, right? I mean who rides in complete silence?" Nonetheless, we would pray together, then ride in total silence - I mean complete silence for about 40 minutes with my head down to avoid any contact, visual or physical.

At that time in my life, I was going through (self-diagnosed) postpartum depression. While at work, I would put on my "happy face" and smile to everyone I'd come across. I would do everything I could to provide excellent customer service to clients and go above and beyond to solve all customer issues. I would get home, however, and all masks were off. I settled in to the real me, the depressed me, the angry me. I practically walked in the door mad. Again, we were living with family, and the thought of them sitting home all day long, with no dinner made by the time we got home was enough to send my blood pressure through the roof. I would also grow agitated from the different mishaps, which involved my babies, because they weren't being closely monitored throughout the day. To top it off, my husband would be outside hanging out across the street with the neighbors, instead of spending quality time with me.

I felt like nothing was going the way I had planned or wanted in my life. I was bitter – *really* bitter. I was the definition of a SAAD woman. This depressive state was one I didn't want to be in, and I couldn't seem to find an escape. So, there I was – stuck, stagnant, trapped, and immovable in this deep dark place called depression, with seemingly no way out.

Drowning in Depression

I knew I was messed up. I knew I was suffering from mental illness, and I was not ashamed to admit it. I just didn't know how to get help. My emotions were spiraling out of control. I tried talking to my husband, but he didn't understand how I felt or what I was experiencing. I wanted to tell my friends and not feel like a bother, but I didn't. There were people I was hoping would rescue me, but they didn't. I was hoping my father would pay attention and save me, but he didn't. I was hoping my sister would recognize the distancing, but she didn't. I was hoping other family members would see the hurt and the pain I was carrying and would be willing to help me – but they didn't. I just needed one person I could trust with my vulnerabilities – one person I could lean on. All I needed was one person to really ask me how I was doing. I mean really, truly, genuinely ask. But they didn't.

I was drowning from the pressure I placed on myself, but too concerned with what others may think or say about me. I was also drowning from the disappointment and unrealistic expectations I set for myself. I wanted so badly for someone to save me. I was even going to the doctor, trying to get answers. Yet the weight just kept getting heavier and heavier. As I was on the verge of a breakdown and wanting to escape, God extended His grace upon me.

My Earthly Angel

One day, I had a vision of me in a room surrounded by darkness. There was one dimly lit beam shining on what appeared to be me, laying down, draped in white. I was laying on a bed in a hospital room – fighting for my life. In that vision, God appeared and whispered to me saying, "My child, you've got to get up from here."

When I saw myself lying in that hospital bed, it was as if God was saying, "If you don't stop stressing, being angry, anxious, and depressed - you are going to end up sick!" From that moment on, I was determined to figure a way out of depression. I started to reflect on all the things that make me happy like music, singing, and dancing. I decided to get back to doing the things I loved and was most passionate about. I chose to start with singing. I put up ads looking for people to meet up with and jam out in a singing session. I was interested in joining a live band, working with a producer, and even forming a group.

Luckily for me, I met an older woman online who was looking to do a few music projects at her in-home studio. She needed someone to do background vocals and I was looking for a place to sing. It seemed like a match made in heaven. For a few months, I worked with her on original songs I had written. We worked really well together.

My creativity and motivation were slowly returning. My passion was reignited, and I started to feel whole again. I felt like I was on top of the world. Unfortunately, the partnership with the producer was short- lived as she stopped returning my emails, calls, or text messages. She literally fell off the face of the earth. While to this day, it's a mystery what happened to her; I truly believe she was my saving grace – my earthly angel. She was the one used by God to help me out of that really dark place in my life, at a time I couldn't see my own way out. God saved me from myself.

My husband didn't fully understand the extent of my illness or the pressure I was feeling during my depression. He would often say, "Just pray about it". Yes, pray about it, and then what? He knew I was taking medication, but he did not understand the seriousness of the situation. I continued my journey out of depression through medical intervention, exercise, and lots of prayer. I even started to lose weight.

Although I really didn't feel up to it, I never stopped being around people. Even when I didn't want to go to church, I kept going! As a result, my self-confidence and hope returned. Before I knew it, I was in a great space mentally and emotionally. Once I was feeling like myself again, my husband noticed the difference. He would tell me that I didn't need the medication and I was fine. Guess What? I agreed, because I was pleased with my progress. My doctor and I devised a plan to slowly stop taking the medication.

Wrong idea!

CHAPTER 8

Anger: The Runaway Train

"Anger is a momentary madness, so control your passion or it will control you."

-G. M. Trevelyan

When I stopped taking my depression medication and tried to live life without any medical intervention, I failed miserably. Once again, I was an angry black woman feeling stressed, burdened, overwhelmed, bitter, and frustrated. I must say, many of the things I would worry about were out of my control, but I couldn't let it go. Slowly the stress, the worry, the overthinking, and fears found their place within my spirit again. This time around, it was worse. I went from depressed to angry - angrier than I had been in the past. In fact, I was angry all the time.

Things would easily frustrate me and cause me to go from 0 to 100 quickly.

Contrary to popular belief, anger is not considered a mental illness. It is, however, a triggering disorder from another issue. Anger is considered a warning sign, indicating one of the following mental health conditions are present: Depression, OCD, alcohol abuse, ADHD,

Oppositional Defiant Disorder, Bipolar Disorder, Intermittent Explosive Disorder, or grief, according to *Healthline*.

When we can't control our anger, we communicate our opinion or express our feelings in a way that may be harmful to ourselves and others. I have come to the realization that I become angry as a result of failed expectations within my relationships – specifically my relationship with my husband and my children.

In all honesty, after my third child, I feel like I lost all patience. Don't get me wrong - I love my children. I enjoy talking with them and teaching them. However, I haven't always had the most patience with them. Is it because I am unhappy with myself? Let's face it, my children are a reflection of me. They are a part of me. They carry personalities, characteristics, and behaviors they got from me. So, could it be that I see so much of myself in them, that it makes me uncomfortable and even fearful about their future physical and mental well-being? If I'm honest, deep down inside, I'm disappointed because I always thought I would be further along in life. My dreams and plans are so far from my reality. I definitely want to teach my children a better way of planning and crushing their goals.

Anger Uncontrolled

Have you ever been so angry, it took you a while to calm down? I had been angry for a long time, partly because I felt like my life was out of control or maybe just out of *my* control. My children were out of control. My family was out of control. My finances were out of control. My living situation was out of control, and my marriage was out of control.

I began to hate myself. I didn't like who I was becoming. Every time I blew up or yelled at the kids, I would always think, "*I am going to make myself sick*". There have been many times I have felt like a crazy person, after yelling at my children. I would try to calm myself down, but the anger and rage were so powerful – I couldn't control it. I feared my children would grow up remembering me as the "mean mommy", in the same way I thought about my mom when I was younger.

As a parent I really tried to manage my reactions, but I was easily frustrated whenever my children wouldn't follow simple instructions. Sometimes, I felt as though they were being defiant on purpose. I would get so angry and could feel the rage boiling under my skin. Since I felt like I wasn't being heard, I sometimes wondered if my family would be better off doing life without me.

Suicide Watch

Allow me to share a story about a time my anger was through the roof and I actually thought about taking my own life. I had just told my husband that I needed some family time and we should hang out with the kids in our room and watch a movie. We have a large California King Bed – so surely the five of us would fit.

During this time, I had been really stressed and full of anxiety from work. I was the only black woman on a team with three other women who did not look like me, doing a job for which I was overqualified. I had more practical on-the-job experience than all of them put together, yet I was expected to perform my duties without error, all the while smiling and meeting potential candidates who would be hired to do the very same job I temporarily held. Needless to say, I was overwhelmed with emotion and really on edge, as a result of what I was experiencing. So, I really needed my family to love on me. I made it a point to be sure I communicated to my husband exactly what I was going through and what I needed.

It was a Saturday night. We were getting things all set up to hang out as a family. The boys had a guest over who was about to leave. Once their company was gone, my oldest son became upset. So, my husband thought it was a good idea to play video games with my son, instead of us all hanging out together. Now, I can totally understand playing one or two games to lift his spirits. But, after a few games, I was livid. I felt my husband didn't care about what I needed or what I was going through at that moment. So again, I locked myself in our bedroom closet. I was so upset, I started having chest pains. I began questioning whether or not I was needed in this world. I seriously contemplated hanging myself right there in our closet. I kept praying that God would ease the pain and take the thoughts away.

For some, I know that scenario seemed a bit drastic. But when you are constantly faced with the same neglect and rejection, you begin to feel like your feelings don't matter. Some people ask the question, "What's the point of being around?" For me the question was, "*What if I killed myself?*"

I was in the closet for at least an hour before the kids tried to come in and say good night, but I ignored their knocks. Hours later, my husband came knocking on the door and I ignored his knocks. I was so pissed at that point. I felt like if he was concerned and if he wanted to get in the door, he could've easily taken off the door handle – but he didn't even try. I was locked in a closet contemplating taking my life, and my husband had no idea. Then I imagined what the morning would be like if I committed suicide. I imagined the police being called, the ambulance coming in, and my kids being traumatized.

God's spirit arose within me and He saw fit that I didn't think about myself at that moment. I thought about my husband, my children, and my family. I imagined not showing up for the high school girls in our student ministry the next morning. I thought about how they needed me. Taking my life would be like not showing up for my children or the students at church. I didn't want to let the students down, let alone, my own children. So, I just laid there in the closet. I thought about a few people I could call to talk me off of the ledge, but it was late and something inside of me just wouldn't let me dial anyone's number. So, there I was locked in my bedroom closet, laying in my own misery the entire night.

The next morning, it was hard to get moving. I had no motivation or inspiration to get up and get dressed. I was definitely tired from not getting any sleep. I was dreading going to church and smiling at everyone, when deep down inside I was hurting.

I pressed my way to church anyway and I am so glad I did. Without me saying a word to anyone about the kind of night I had, the youth minister decided to do something a little different on this particular Sunday. Instead of praying a general prayer over the students, right at the end of Praise and Worship, he decided to call all servant leaders to the front. He wanted to cover the volunteers who served in the student ministry with prayer because he realized we too are faced with life's challenges just like many of the students. He started praying and my heart was heavy.

As he was praying, he specifically prayed against the spirit of suicide. I stood there, eyes shut, head down, and tears rolling down my face. It was God telling me I made the right decision by not taking my life and pressing my way to church because someone in the Kingdom just prayed for me.

There was no way the youth minister knew what I suffered the night before, but God knew and He knew I needed that prayer.

I share this story with you because, like me, so many people are hurting. Many are walking around smiling on the outside, appearing to have it all together, but on the inside, they are falling apart. When we sense something is not right, or we feel like someone is stressed, depressed, or even overwhelmed, let's take a moment to genuinely ask how they are doing. If we don't feel like we can provide empathy and prayer at that moment, let's find someone who can. I'm so glad God kept me that night and His grace overpowered the spirit of suicide.

CHAPTER 9

Journey To Healing

"'For I will restore health to you and heal you of your wounds,' says the Lord"

Jeremiah 30:17 (NKJV)

Have I always had my own faith? Absolutely not. My faith in God has not always been strong, but it has grown and continues to do so. Like many of you, I relied on the faith of my parents and my grandparents, when I was younger. I used to think God was disappointed with me because of the decisions I made. At the age of 15, I made a personal choice to accept Jesus into my heart and become my Lord and Savior, but I know His spirit has always lived within me.

His Spirit Lives Within Me

One Sunday in 1995, the late Rev. Dr. Leroy Johnson preached a sermon that spoke to my spirit so much that at 15-years-old, I got out of my seat and walked down the middle aisle of the church during the call of discipleship. I stood in line behind other members with a heavy heart, dealing with confusion, low self-esteem, and a sense of worthlessness. I'd suffered a lifelong war in my mind, my spirit, and my emotions. It was time for my deliverance.

By the time I reached Rev. Johnson, my hands were clamped together, intertwined in a praying position with my head hung low. I felt so ashamed. I felt unworthy. I felt dirty. I felt guilty. I felt regretful and sorry. I wanted so much for God to help me through everything I was going through. I wanted God to help me be a better person and save me from myself, because my life had been spiraling out of control, even as a teenager.

As God's earthly vessel placed his hands upon my head and began to pray for me, I immediately became overwhelmed by the spirit and started crying uncontrollably as I dropped to my knees. Rev. Johnson told me that the spirit of God lived in me and God had a purpose for my life. He said God would use me and my gifts for the upbuilding of His kingdom. He told me to keep trusting God. It was that encounter that began my personal relationship with God - not a perfect relationship without sin - but a genuine relationship nonetheless.

Growing In Faith

As I grew older, I started fasting and praying on my own to hear God's voice for clarity and direction and to receive the blessings he had for me. I began worshipping God throughout my home - in the bedroom, living room, kitchen, and even in the car. I remember walking the halls and praying over my home and my family. I realized I didn't have to be in the church building to worship and pray.

I began trusting God to do what He felt was possible in my life. I never really trusted God to do the impossible, until it was time to try and purchase our first home. I could not see past our current situation. With our measly bank account and poor credit, I knew the only way we could get approved for a loan to purchase our very first home, was God. There was nothing we could've done in our own might to get approved for a home loan. We barely had $1,000 to secure the lot let alone the down payment.

My husband and I fasted and prayed because we needed God to intervene and help us through the process. We prayed together every day on our drive to work. We fasted from morning until early afternoon. I remember driving up to Sacramento and picking up the key to our prospective new home so we could check on the building process. The home was almost ready for closing and move- in. We sat on the floor just inside the front door, held hands, and prayed over our home. We believed in God for a miracle and He did not disappoint. We couldn't believe we were approved for the loan. We trusted God throughout our entire home purchase process, and He blessed us with a beautiful, brand-new home. God blew my mind. I couldn't believe we had purchased our first home. I am so thankful for that moment of stepping out on faith and really trusting God in an impossible situation.

Just as I stepped out on faith for our home purchase, I did the same thing when I was diagnosed with breast cancer. Because of my spiritual growth and personal relationship with God, my diagnosis didn't break me. I believed if God saved my mother from a heart attack, saved my aunt from breast cancer, brought my brother out of a coma, saved my Nana from a burning house *and* blessed her to experience 99 wonderful years on this earth, I knew He could do it for me.

I was able to activate the spirit of discernment and the spirit of wisdom in making critical decisions about my care. I knew that in order for me to be completely healed, I had to trust God and tap into His vision and purpose for my life. I had to set myself free from the S.A.A.D. (Stress, Anger, Anxiety, and Depression) Woman Syndrome. I had been in bondage for years and it was time to be set free. I owed it to myself, my husband, and my children.

I began to pray and ask God to help me through the stress, the anxiety, the anger, and the depression. I needed HIS help to become a better version of myself. I needed His help to be the example I wanted my children to see. I needed God's grace and mercy to heal from past hurts, disappointments, and failures. Only He could help me be a vessel in His kingdom and help spread the word about His healing power. I would need Him to help me carry out His purpose and vision for my life. I grew tired of trying to live on my terms. I was tired of trying to make things happen and fall in line the way *I* saw fit. Instead, I approached God naked and unafraid – unapologetically, asking Him to save me and truly be the Lord of my life.

Total Submission

With lifted hands, I surrendered wholeheartedly and asked God to use me for the uplifting and building of his Kingdom. However, He must have thought that for me to be able to lead people to Christ, I needed some credibility – hence my story of surviving breast cancer. From the moment I received my diagnosis, I knew God was preparing me for my greater purpose in this life. He must have felt that for me to reach the lost and give hope to the hopeless, I needed to personally experience what it was like to have hope in a hopeless situation and be found in a time when I was lost.

After much-needed self-reflection, I came to terms with all of the challenges, issues, and distractions, over the years, that have stood in the way of me fulfilling my true purpose. I came to the realization that I have suffered for a long time from the S.A.A.D Woman Syndrome (Stress, Anxiety, Anger, and Depression). As I was in the middle of the fight of my life, I knew that in order for me to survive breast cancer and fully recover, I needed to heal holistically, and this included being healed from past hurts and disappointments.

I understood stress, anxiety, anger, and depression not only causes certain health issues, but it exacerbates them. I was determined to change how I viewed myself, my life, my husband, my children, my marriage, and my family. I reprioritized what was important and what wasn't worth my time, attention, and energy.

I let some things go, in order to move forward. My mindset evolved. I began trusting God and seeking Him more, while I was in the fight. The more I leaned on Him for strength, the more I knew my journey was for a purpose. My suffering was not in vain. I survived on purpose *for* a purpose, and I am determined to fulfill God's purpose for my life. I had to tell myself that I was worth fighting for and I had to remember that I asked God to use me for the uplifting of His kingdom. I had to remember He saved me from myself so many times. God saw me through rejection, neglect, molestation, exploitation, stress, anger, anxiety, and depression. I figured the least I could do was share my journey, my struggles, and my testimony with the world and tell of His goodness and His healing power to help someone else.

CHAPTER 10

Finding Czarinaty

"Peace is the result of retraining your mind to process life as it is, rather than as you think it should be."

-Wayne W. Dyer

New Identity

I had to go back, reintroduce myself, and remind myself of who I am and whose I am. I had to *find* myself because I truly lost sight of my true identity. Like many of us often do, I lost myself after marriage, and even more when I had children. I lost a portion of myself when I lost my mother and probably the biggest portion of myself when I was diagnosed with cancer. I allowed the SAAD woman syndrome to take over my life.

New Strategy

Since my diagnosis, my faith has grown tremendously and I trust God on a new level. I no longer depend on people for love, peace, or happiness. I depend on God. This journey has taught me to stop waiting on others to create my sense of peace. Rather, depend on God's peace and God's love. Then take ownership and protect it. I have learned to love myself by putting myself first. In addition to loving myself, I've concluded it is important for me to love others the way I want to be loved - exercising compassion, patience, and kindness. Exercising kindness makes me feel better. I have also learned staying physically active and eating healthier has given me more energy to carry out my daily tasks.

As I continue my journey to peace and serenity, I have implemented a few strategies that have helped me to maintain my peace of mind. I have become less worried about the opinions of others and no longer allow the distractions of my own negative self-talk stand in the way of my purpose. As a result, I refuse to live by society's standards. I set my own standards and live according to God's word. Therefore, my perception of success has changed. I do not believe success is having financial wealth. I believe success is achieved when one discovers their passion and purpose, then walks in their purpose with passion.

Now that I recognize my stressors and triggers of anxiety, I am in a better position to control and manage my stress. I will continue to communicate how I feel, rather than hope and wish someone already knows my thoughts. I will continue to speak up and speak out, because I have so much to give and share with the world. I will continue to be confident in myself and my abilities. Everything I need to be my best self is already within me – I just have to recognize it.

God has already blessed me with the knowledge, patience, wisdom, and resources I need to carry out His purpose, and I pray He will continue to lead me in the right direction.

Lastly, in order to protect my peace, I must not react to every situation or circumstance. I must also face my fears and accept my imperfections, this includes healing from past hurts. When protecting my peace, I must be confident in my ability to shift the atmosphere, or simply change my environment.

In closing, I'd like to offer some practical advice based on the many invaluable lessons I've learned. If you are currently stressed, full of anger, full of anxiety, feeling overwhelmed, or depressed, I hope you'll take a chapter from my book and learn to love yourself enough to accept your feelings and acknowledge that it's okay not to be okay. I pray you'll find the courage to tell someone how you are feeling and ask for help. I hope you'll seek God for the strength and courage you'll need to change your situation and your mindset. If you are taking care of a family member or friend, do all you can to give them the care, attention, and love they need. If you are currently faced with a traumatic sickness, illness, disease, or situation, be sure to set your mind on things that are positive, as well as those things (and people) that give you hope, joy, and peace.

Now Ask Me - Who Am I?

My name is Czarina. Today, if you ask me what my name means, here is my reply:

I am a Queen, created in God's image. I was created to be a light in a dark world and spread peace amongst God's people. I am a woman of strength and resilience. I have the power to remain calm in the midst of chaos and be the peace in the middle of a storm.

I do not share this story to paint a picture of pity or distaste. It's not easy to share all of the "not so pretty" aspects of life. However, it's not about being pretty - it's about trusting God, healing, and finding peace. So, I share this story because it's my truth. Every lesson, every relationship, every heartache, and every traumatic event I've experienced has made me the woman I am today. I boldly and fearlessly share my story not only to prove you are not alone, but to also prove you, too, can overcome. I believe my breast cancer journey and my story of total and complete healing will definitely help someone who is going through, getting ready to go through, or coming out of a scarring experience.

Before I conclude, please know my husband is a great man, a great father and loyal friend. He is not perfect. Neither am I. Neither are the members of our family. Neither are you. In fact, nobody in this world is perfect. So yes, we've had some imperfect moments, but it will never change the way I feel about him. He has been my rock! He has sacrificed so much to ensure our family had a roof over our heads, food on the table, and clothes on our backs. When I lost my job, my husband worked two sometimes three jobs a day, without any complaints.

I especially want to thank my Sisters-in-Love, Mrs. Dawn Smith and Mrs. Dana Rolling, for sacrificing their time during the time of my surgery. You both showed up and helped out at a really critical time. We didn't have to worry about anything, and for that I am forever grateful!

To my husband, the one who played an irreplaceable role in my breast cancer journey, I honor you. I love you. I can't imagine having to go through this journey without you. We have definitely had to face a few storms, but we made it through - TOGETHER! I can honestly say we've had more amazing days than crazy days. You are not just an amazing husband who has sacrificed so much, you are an AMAZING father to our beautiful boys. You have loved me at times I didn't love myself. You have been loyal and so supportive, with the exception of football season.

(Smile) Thank you so much for allowing me to share my story. Thank you for staying by my side and staying all in, at times when others would've checked out.

To my readers, I can honestly say I have found myself, and I have found peace. I am at peace with myself, my marriage, my children, my past, and my future. I'm eternally grateful for all of my experiences, lessons and trials. They have all been instrumental in my journey to find PEACE and CZARINATY. May God Bless you on the journey to finding yours!

Notes

1. *Common Causes of Stress & Their Effect on Your Health*. (n.d.). WebMD. Retrieved April 10, 2020 from https://www.webmd.com/balance/guide/causes-of-stress%231#2.
2. Mayo Clinic Staff. (2019, March 19). *Chronic stress puts your health at risk*. Mayo Clinic. https://www.mayoclinic.org/healthylifestylpe/stress-management/indepth/stress/art-20046037.
3. Razzetti, G. (2018, October 24). *Live Your Life for You, Not to Please Expectations*. Psychology Today. Retrieved May 30, 2020 from https://www.psychologytoday.com/us/bl

og/the-adaptive-mind/201810/live-yourlife-you-not-please-expectations.

4. Santos-Longhurst, A. (2019, February 4). *Anger Issues: Symptoms, Causes, Diagnosis, and Management*. Healthline. Retrieved March 16, 2020 from https://www.healthline.com/health/anger-issues#treatment.

THANK YOU!

Thank you so much for taking the time to read my story. The writing process has been very therapeutic. I pray you were blessed and inspired to begin your personal journey to peace. Thank you for joining me on my...

Journey to Peace & Czarinaty.